THANK YOU
SO MUCH
I LOVE
YOU
HUMANITY
ROBOT

UP SOUTH

ROBERT LASHLEY

a division of

SMALL DOGGIES PRESS

Portland, Oregon

SMALL DOGGIES PRESS
a division of Small Doggies Omnimedia
smalldoggiesomnimedia.com

Up South
poetry by Robert Lashley

SMALL DOGGIES PRESS © 2017
1ST PRINTING.
MARCH 28, 2017

ISBN: 978-0-9848744-9-1

Printed in the United States of America
10 · 9 · 8 · 7 · 6 · 5 · 4 · 3 · 2 · 1

Small Doggies trade paperback edition, March 2017
Up South, Copyright 2017. • All Rights Reserved.

Published by Small Doggies Press, Portland, OR.

No part of this book may be reproduced or transmitted by any means, electronic or mechanical, including photocopying, recording, or by any information storage and retrieval system, without permission, in writing from the copyright owner, except for a reviewer, who may quote brief passages in a review or within critical articles.

Small Doggies Press: www.SMALLDOGGIESPRESS.COM

Edited by *Carrie Seitzinger*.
Cover Art by *Matty Byloos*.
Cover Design by *Matty Byloos & Olivia Croom*.
Interior Layout by *Olivia Croom*.
Author Photo by *David Blair*.
Type set in ITC Bookman and **ITC Clearface**.

Contents

Frisked on Fraser and Woburn Suicide Blues 1

Abandoned Hip Hop Activist Youth Center,
Hilltop, February 3

Mrs. Mcdaniels Tends Her Winter Beets
(as the Block Gets too Fucking Hot) 5

Elders Rage at the Water Spirits After a Shootout . . 6

That Time Auntie Set Her Broom on Fire
and Started Searching for Her Lost Boy 7

From the City Bus That Took My Black Ass
to School, 4:51AM 8

To the Boys Who Growl at Street Harassers
to Get Them off They Momma's Back 9

Uncle Washes His Niece's Feet
(After a Busted Wedding) 10

New Jerk Dancer Funeral Procession 11

Said the Self-Taught Fresh Out Nigga
to the Grandbaby He Made a Book Nook for. 12

Elegy for a Skipping Circle (a Block in Front
of First Baptist and a Piru Set Trip) 1992 13

Blues for John Amos 15

To Thomas, on the Day He Found God
and Apologized for Making Me Give Him Head. 17

Notes on Koch's Noah's Thank Offering 18

Icarus Asks Me for Swisher Sweets at 7-11 19

The Death of Spartacus on the Strip:
Elders Watching the Holmes-Ali Fight. 21

Pyrrhic Victory at the Corner Exhibition Match . . .24

L.L., a Mile From That Long Beach Restaurant,
After One of My Breakdowns 25

If That Deacon Talks Shit About Your Tats Again,
I'll Cut Him and Write My Prison Memoirs. 27

If the Revolution Comes, You Niggas Better
Not Fuck With Our Cat 29

The Husband of the First Woman Punished
by the Laws of Moses 31

Portrait of a Practice Boy Spitting at the Gods,
Hours After Thomas Finished 32

The Funeral Procession for Aunt Helen
at Her Favorite Swap Meet 34

The 15th and L Arsonist Who Threatened to
Smoke Me if I Snitched on Him, 1994. 35

A Father's 20th Funeral Anniversary 37

Old Shermed Pirus Who Struggle
to See the Sun in Winter 39

When the OG Took the Fall for Once
(Then Realized It Was His Last) 41

Portrait of an Ex-Piru, Right Outside the Mall,
With His Daughters Fixed High Heels 42

Young Elder Who Makes a Scrunchie
on the Sidewalk. 43

L. L., 1993 44

Uncle Moe Dresses Big Momma for Church, the
Morning After One of Dad's Tantrums 45

Pops Tries to Sell Big Momma's Special Pot
for That Stuff 46

On the Day He Lost His Religion and Sobriety. . . . 47

The Time He Wanted to Talk to Some Niggas
at the Pier About Being a Kingpin 49

Burning Unc's Poetry Papers 50

Song for Mrs. Eulalah. 52

The Gun Solstice: An Anti-Journey 54

Drake's Progress 60

L. L., April 7th, 3:17PM (TW) 61

Visit to the House After "The Accident" 62

Portrait of a Ferret Among a Divorcing Couple
in a Gentrified Startup 65

The Revolution Cannot Hold You:
Freshman Breakup at the Amtrak. 66

To the Couple, the Tree of Life Lives in Metaphor . . 67

When God Lets My Body Be 68

Frisked on Fraser and Woburn Suicide Blues
(with a nod to Yeats)

"Or does it explode?"
—Langston Hughes, "What Happens to a Dream Deferred"

Or does it escape you?
Does it leave—in the quiet—
in the sudden declines
of September—by synonyms
of nature and circles
of cars and men who plead
your body like the drums—
men who plead your blood
long after your skin lies
in its veneer of matter.

Does it leave with your body
transformed to a swan
with grit wings beating
and a staggering gate
with webs and napes
and terrifying fingers
as your body gets limp by the window?

And after they finish
will the sun have too much light?
Will the breeze and all its subtexts
violate your space
and will the willow trouble your mind?

Will the evergreens—fixed
in their portable promised lands—color
a life you'll never have?

Abandoned Hip Hop Activist Youth Center, Hilltop, February
(a parody of "Short Speech to My Friends"
by Amiri Baraka)

The street lamps are circuited northern stars.
They flicker over first sheens of hanging paint flecks
and empty building particles.
They twitch over left gear, boxes, and renovations
on top of each other.
     Crack! Crack! Crack! Crack!

They spotlight contracts in tatters.
They highlight black words
of old student letters
but cannot not make sentences cohere.
They illuminates mix tapes:
shared beats and creations,
visible only by tape signatures.
     Crack! Crack! Crack! Crack!

Consoles and termites
are bodied and silhouetted
on top of themselves and each other.
Smoke layers metastasize
as a corner store crew
conjures the imagism in firecrackers.
     Crack! Crack! Crack! Crack!

The death of woke art is never tender.
The strings of people's picked clean fingers

never touch.
The width of its autumns makes wider avenues blank
and the night is a concrete apparition.
New highways in the distance
disappear in layered fogs.
New buildings below are a mosaic of dirt light
and noises exaggerate in lack of mass.
Windows assume the perversity of distance
and all who are left here are moving.
    Crack! Crack! Crack! Crack!

Mrs. Mcdaniels Tends Her Winter Beets (as the Block Gets too Fucking Hot)

On solstice,
the winter sprouts announce themselves
in colors of brown and blue.

The sprout is the altar
for the OG's communion suit,
the defrosted memorial
for iced out cousins
in various chases of crystal,
the new life in faith
in the mass of detritus
and the ends/beginnings of December.

The day designs itself in frail rises.
Light abets the shades of dope boys who travel
past the blossoms of stems of rock pipes.
Light contrasts with a cop car's crocodile wail
as it passes over block after block.
Light hits brown faces
on tracks and commotions
that intersect and intersect.

On solstice, winter's sprouts
are an underground windmill.
Seeds from red clay reimagine the past
and protect her from tribes
and recall.

Elders Rage at the Water Spirits After a Shootout

Reflection, on the lake
is a ripple that eats
then spits out an outline of the woods.
The women in black dip their old tambourines
then blur away from it.
The old men tie their suits into knots
then blur away from it.
The people join and move their hands
to deny his name in the cold.
                      "The water spirit brought us.
    "The water spirit will not bring us home."
They wash the memory of blood in ice
and cry power in the darkness.
    "The water spirit will not bring us home."
Hums turn to shouts and chants rewoven
and moans play in scale with the squirrel bounce.
    "The water spirit will not bring us home."
Frogs jump a beat back from their hand claps.
Night bugs swarm but cannot trace steps
in an array of burying grounds
of shadows and spirits in the water.
The juba clap is the overriding veil
of sirens and funeral pyres.
The gun shot at night is the eleventh plague
so they part this iteration of the sea.
                      "The water spirit brought us.
    "The water spirit will not bring us home."

That Time Auntie Set Her Broom on Fire and Started Searching for Her Lost Boy

A rainbow sign in twig, it becomes
a solar system—wood—metal—burning
Straw—a centrifugal lamp that draws
and compels people from the trap line.
> *Boo man, boo man, get back from me.*
> *Boo man, boo man, get back.*

Around it, runner boys stop then pedal
faster than the speed of her relight.
> *Boo man, boo man get back from me.*

Church folk go outside to her, then throttle.
Their feet fail them—in grime—on the ground
their gators and house shoes illuminate in sheens
outrageous and ghetto-fabulously-austere
> *Boo man, boo man get back from me.*

In fire, she shines on old men's seasons
of witches and white flake ravaged skin,
of monkeys that ride the demented twins
in victim and victimizers minds
fire-mirror in their triplicates of rocks.
> *Boo man, boo man, get back.*

Around it, she throws rice on the ground.
Fiends kneel down in their chase-toasts and worships.
They kneel on the jagged damp of the concrete
to a blind god in smoke altars of off-white.
They chase the damp ground with a joy seldom seen
as they try to smoke their piece by piece.
> *Boo man, boo man, get back from me.*
> *Boo man, boo man, get back.*

From the City Bus That Took My Black Ass to School, 4:51AM
(with the first two lines as an homage to Wislawa Szymborska's "Travel Elegy")

Everything is yours but on loan.
Nothing in young memory to hold
but semi-fictive sermons of bondage.
Dreams of deliverance are in the blank spaces
between lunch bags, promised lands, and Walkmen.
Dawn is messy, cold, and punishing
but it moves as it needs to move.

In the iteration of the morning train
lights flash only as prequel.
Cars drive slow or jaggedly kinetic
in streets that feel like highways.
Black turns to blue turned to slant shades of grey
as division lines from plain glass blur.
Vision comes to offices, churches and strip malls
empty as Monday cathedrals.

In the predawn, Beulah Land
is fixed and fluid.
The view of the finish line
before the weight of the journey
is illusory in county bus blocks.
The memory of buckets kicked, lived, and cast
are invisible, yet harder than matter.
In wilderness, the outside is a window mélange
of a hundred rainbow signs.

To the Boys Who Growl at Street Harassers to Get Them off They Momma's Back

"never look the hotcomb in the teeth, queens"
yet the eviction notice is a starless gyre
the first project death is not ice or fire
but in exodus from concrete and shelter.
Men speak of royals and drink their ripple.
Nationhood is a mask that has no face
to the kingmakers of the block and corner
though Sundays is no rest to azure pharos.
The light shows they live in outlines
fallen gladiator-boys among frocked deacons.
In the tatters of invisible shields
they holler and make noise in invisible fields
yet the rent is realer than space.
Makeshifted pantsuits they nip at and splice
in their mind, so your mouth cuts
their channels. In low rabid roars
radiate madness on the madness
in untreated thugs fevers and dreams
Their surfeit splendors into sounds
fling at the seams of makeup defenses
make your mouth the bus wailing walls.

Uncle Washes His Niece's Feet (After a Busted Wedding)

Now is past god and his altar light Kente's,
past surfaces of shells—of brooms and their frames,
past bonds—legal and in tradition—decayed.
        Sister, let me soak your bunions.
Now is past ministers (but not ministers of spices),
past the roots and the fruits of exodus screwed
       then processed in generations of rituals.
Now is not for procession but peelers and tub salts.
        Little sister, come and sit with me.
Now, past the moment of the boyman's rut
and men who speak of youth and nothing but
while oats seed a poison to their face,
he sits with his bucket and new Epsom bag
       and clears if not clarifies myth.
At the wedding now, only sulfur is truth.
Commitment is a yoke that bears two weights
so in the middle of the mosque she eats pork.
Spikes hit in the heel—then the head—
       then the heart
and the red bucket is a hiding place.
        Little sister, let me soak them bunions.
Love is a sign here that has no face
and a hotplate is her only commitment.
        Little sister, the heart is a moving tent.
        Little sister, let me soak them bunions.

New Jerk Dancer Funeral Procession

Beyond names of love (or love after love).
we move across getting up specters of corners
that hover past our lineup.
We re-apply cadences, quarters and times
decoded and recorded from the drum beat.
> *Let us leap the block.*

The milk crate table has lasting arms.
The concrete below is memory transfigured
beyond the matter of the needle
beyond all temporary arrested threads
shouldered in aged steadied vinyl.
> *Let us leap the block.*

Beyond gray, we pray in measures of feet:
a stride along paved tedious journey,
and traverses through earth burroughed pitfall,
a step on the one past the clutter,
a good foot on the one and never the other.
> *Let us leap the block.*

In the circle, delta's and darkened corners
are cycled if not spun.
Juice glass altars catch the spirit
on the basin of their welcome table.
Threshing floors are re-chalked and colored
in calls and response to concrete.
Beyond all form in stride we meet
> *Let us leap the block.*

Said the Self-Taught Fresh Out Nigga to the Grandbaby He Made a Book Nook for

Your wisdom will have no clocks, love.
Your strength of street knowledge
will have no colors or tracks
and the ankh won't put a price on you
in a protectorate of steel.
Plates to the temple I will build to the east
my church to your future beyond my past.

Here is a structure rebuilt from a blood dream.
My life is a structure rebuilt from my blood dream.
Here, what has been undone in beams
I cannot redo but make an altar for.
In irons, casts, and a wood marble floor
I'll erect what I tore with my Tims.

Dear, I build but don't worship me
Prayers—like designs—aren't translatable
They do not judge or gage.
They disappear as restitution
their layers and codes a table
you can decipher in the dust.
Quadrants are fixed
but your mind is infinite.
        Yes I will shut up and finish.

Elegy for a Skipping Circle (a Block in Front of First Baptist and a Piru Set Trip) 1992
(with a nod to Dylan Thomas)

I.
I see the girls of summer on the concrete.
They float above tides and tidings broomed and barren.
They set no home by harvest, freeze the beat.
There, past the heat of winter bloods
they clap together with an unpetty pace
beyond macks and Mother Mary.

The boys of light jewels are curdlers for that money.
Lines of lines freaks form and divide
for jacks in darken corners and kilo hives
in tandem—yet disarrayed—are zombie like waves
of young mad dawgs initiated
there—from the moon rocks—unfrigid threads
of taps and jumps unfurl the nerves
Gun-shy church ladies drown all with gospel.
Shut-ins peek disappear under the railing.

From boys shall men of nothing
wander as they wonder on seeds
that lame the air of boys and their heaters.
Old man around them re-dream menageries
in ripple and their underpants.

II.
Yet seasons are met and challenged
in blues and blue dreams

where—punctual as scales—they hang brick moons
There in the night—the contours of skins
of young gangsters
run a ragged teardrop train downward.

In razors, dark deniers minister and father
razors begat new war marks
and lifetime's signs.
Through snot in their chest, screens form
harden, and vivify
to show their future in claims—
in bonds and chains and sets.

In spring they cross a bic up on forehead.
Hate on "hoes" among bloods and ballers
and mortgage their hards in a bid
to be unseen lords.
Light dims a misbegotten sunset in late September.
The young boys move, but cannot move toward home.

III.
Extensions of wool and Woolworth snares
contrast in repetition and memory;
strands are perpendicular ceremonies
that turn back burning lands,
that set a fragile field of men,
deadbeat lectures in concrete wilderness.
        Church playas and macks
macks   macks   lean in the back   back   back
cadillacs wide   wide   wide   we gonna
die   die   die

Blues for John Amos
(I flip a line from Shelley's "To a Skylark")

Teach us, TBS spirit
we cable your manner.
From apartment to apartment.
From cord ply to cord ply
to which rooms will allow
for the evidence of niggas unseen.

Higher still and higher
from the firmaments of the steps
and the rusted railing iron
we mimic you like a science.
To the fluid, vivid motion
on the glass and in the screenshot
we practice your demeanor.
For the timeshare and hour
we will sacrifice by foil
and hookup to see your face.

In the golden light pole
of sunken suns
the old heads below want to tax us.
Rituals or oblivion
or oblivions surrogate in zippers
linger in the antennas unseen hourglass.
We seek refuge in your presence,
you, a voice, a swagger.
Your manner upon men
44 minutes on the hour
those not preempted by braves game.

Teach us, TBS John Henry.
Teach us half the stability
that the act must know.
The shows in minutes will soon be done
and we will have to leave
and go down again.

To Thomas, on the Day He Found God and Apologized for Making Me Give Him Head

Bitter is the bread of your word on Antioch,
Bitter the taste—bitter the kneading—
bitter the loaves yet far bitter the feeding
    Go back home, lost son, go home.
Bitter is the song told over in glory,
told on the times of other boys' souls,
told on our back and the backs of our skulls
    Go back home, lost son, go home.
Bitter is the prologue—your call—your response
your spirit that suffers by proxy.
Your spirit's not the only one to sacrifice his body
    Go back home, lost son go home.
Bitter is your David—your brown skinned Saul—
your cross and your redemption plan.
Your pleas here are hollow: I am only a man.
    Go back home, lost son, go home.
Bitter is the sound of your new jubilee.
Stained is the soul claps—stained their tongues—
stained to the everlasting, passed over and gone
    from redemption in dirty church rivers.
Bitter is the mouth—still—of what you severed.
    Go back home, lost son, go home.

Notes on Koch's Noah's Thank Offering

The canvas is empty and his temper stops.
The palms that would never wait or give
are erased from questions of roots.
Sediments from the dirt to the word are milled
among prologues of mass by the water.

The rainbow, by the bank, is the lost father of faith.
And faith is work's beat and broken brother.
And work, in prayer, the searched synonym of truth
in the hearth on the calf of the seeker.
The people come to the altar from the tent
and the doubter comes barefoot for their feelers.

And mercy, in this peculiar bent,
disperses in angst to a million rivers,
and people—from the arks—give worship what
and which manner that they were spared;
he yearns, this shepherd in a transfer of world
to believe past the visuals of the drought.
The ox man, the miller from the dirt from the word
strains to sacrifice as survivors shout
>   *Save me, o who praise the water.*
>   *Save me from the misnamed sea.*
>   *The water spirits are not mother,*
>   *Death's taking a hold of me.*
>   *Death's taking a hold of me.*

Icarus Asks Me for Swisher Sweets at 7-11

I did not see her in flight or morning.
I did not stand her harps or trumpets
or anything in my getting up day.
I traded the dreams we made on the ground
for my dream to be a god in the sky
(it was a glided Gethsemane).
Hell is immortality without a net.
Immortality is a moon that never sets
after a million Sunday suns.

What was more important in the clouds
to my zest for joy unseen?
What unseen lord lineated my wings
and made them more important than our broom?
What made them more important than our leaps
through earth bound walls and beams?
What-in the light-was far more desirable
than the beads of sweat in our dreams?

Once we salved our scars on the ground,
the fields that moved from space we tided
and stole away from lashes and bounders.
Once we stilled the weevil in stole away hours
and made nothing more important than our clay.
Once we spun and made a world
        and then I flew away.

Why, boy, why should she have not kept moving?

My funeral band should have been dusted.
My procession was better off bare and emptied
in a taxonomy of heartbreak and loss;
A mourners' row of upturned plots
for living graves of swords and shields.
Hope brought her no feathers in ruby red fields
and memory gave her no balms.
Why should she mourn me in the memory of flight
when my rails meant more than her arms?

The Death of Spartacus on the Strip: Elders Watching the Holmes-Ali Fight
(I lift two lines from "The Hollow Men")

I.
Rib Plates become homegoing wreaths
the memorex has told over a thousand deaths
as old men kneel and clap and hum
tribunal lines—fades in screen become
the gallows in the middle of the palace
        "And Holmes continues... systematic, methodical purposeful"
The ring is the end of every revolution.
The young guard jabs
with direct weeping eyes
then crosses him with the length of his wingspan.
The slave soldier crosses to death's sister kingdom
as lights put out heat but no sun.
        His hands no longer busy
        his feet no longer swift.

Tonight, the ropes produce no magic
the young blood is the ax man cometh.
The bell ends a fugue of punches and punches
then renders his silence a sound.
The rollers that leave and the fans that cannot move
renders his silence a sound.
Cries that form concentric circles from the screen
render his silence a sound.
        Brothers, brothers, niggas, niggas
        let's go to the burying ground.

II.
Below the hill, the nelson building Is a shadow.
The sea harbor's work is a fetid smell.
and store ruins are crackhead temples.
Harbor roughnecks pain is chopped and proof
in the second life in flickers in the walls.
> *Brothers, brothers, niggas, niggas*

In the back of the bodega
the elders rewitness:
not to testify to art or squalor
but to claim his name in the side room,
to honor all old pug's upturned graves
and fleeting memories in the tapes.
Tapes show their repeated rainbow sign
through smokers and Saturday cathedrals,
their witness to the sacrifice by glittery hearth
of death-strewn means and ends,
their rite—through contract—to quickly transcend
pyric ends that linger after the TV.
> *Brothers, brothers, niggas, niggas*
> *let's go to the burying ground.*

III.
Lights that transformed his life to a myth
transform myth to a landscape of the physical.
> *"Angelo is telling the referee to stop it..."*

The tape is a fractal to a thousand Sisyphean deaths
yet the old men stay solemn in the ritual.
The old screen loops, then fuzzes then fuzzes
yet they sit in spell of the audio
> *"Bundini is arguing with him.*
> *Brothers, brothers, niggas, niggas"*

Lights fray, and the echo of crowds lay still
a hush over the makeshift bungalow
from the meat room to the bar.
The old men pass the Boones farm and scarves
in the pocket of the bootleg Gunicelli's
they got at the swap meet.
The broadcast—frayed—becomes a jittery chant.
> *"He would not... he would not give in, Angelo Dundee.*
> *He cared about his fighter! Too much!*
>> *The way Eddie Futch cared about Joe Frazier! Too much!*
> *In 1975 in Manilla! Too Much!"*

In Vegas, the gladiator's life is a funeral.
The old men kneel their head in benediction
and the continued sacrifice of the body.
>> *Let's go to the burying ground.*
>> *Let's go to the burying ground.*

Pyrrhic Victory at the Corner Exhibition Match

The boymen gather at the pavement hall.
The rock man's squeal is a disjointed bell
and altar call for circles and good seats.
Tremors rearranged in the fronts of skulls
looped in hooks, right crosses and jabs.
In pistons so heavy disoriented and dulled
yet on contact drew oil on your noses
your eardrum—your eyelashes they hated
your lips they threatened with copper wires
to come in by alleys and corners
your mouth so intimate with drawls of blood
made by insertion, force and knuckles.
    "Fight! Be a man."
Swallow it down the kindle of your lungs!
Brave through the need to cry for your moms,
then see him, beet red, as the bell ringed;
then see him and think, "In other lives
we could have been best friends and homies."
And now you are on the backs of several,
starter champions in starter jerseys,
carriers of stench and sweat and blood
too thick for breath or recusal
with glory, not for you but your whippings,
your blood trials by fire with you ahead
the cards stacked so heavy in your favors,
Don't look at him, there, alone from his crews.
And the men with him aside the corner.

L.L., a Mile From That Long Beach Restaurant, After One of My Breakdowns

The wave tries to pull us
over the neon of her tattoo.
The wave tries to pull us
but she laughs at it.

The restaurant comes together—
then melts—then congeals again—
then disintegrates in the salts
that dance with her.

The broke beats of my heart
are untombed in her arms.
                A tossed salad is not a metaphor.

Outside, darkness colors in its pace
but cannot shade the light of her neck
the unseen nest of her breast and back
defy all logic and color
defy the eternal night of other
nightmares transformed into metaphor.
A tossed salad is not a metaphor
but a dish up on that floor.

The marshes decorate
themselves around us.
They feather her hair
and the pearls of my sweat.
They migrate from the confines

of file and phylum
for the chance to lay right beside us.

>A tossed salad is not a metaphor
>but a dish upon that floor
>but the ground unto the sea is boiling.

"*We cannot run to rock, love
for the rock has never hid us.
We cannot run to the river
for the surplus of skeletons
but let us lay down at the sea.*

*We will make the great world spin.
May the skylines flip.
May the world be disjointed
as I fling my hair.
May everything but us seem human error
outside the gate of our arms.*

"*My love, may we cut across the shoreline.
May we silhouette the ebbs,
the flora and fauna.
May we defy the defining lines.
May we make the currents our jesters.
Let us stem and remake the median
...........that is ours and ours alone.*

*The wave tries to pull us over the neon of her breast.
The wave tries to pull us but she laughs at it.*

If That Deacon Talks Shit About Your Tats Again, I'll Cut Him and Write My Prison Memoirs (or, Two Hoodlums Hiding in the Shed With Luther)

Your columns and crosses—
your errant birds—
your neon patches and hidden words:
I know no gods but them now.
      I'd be a fool.... to ev...ver... change

Let the sun and moon
have their contradiction of followers.
Let the matchmen that strain and strain to sketch you
costume image for facts.
Life—in deeds—and words—and acts
is the syllogism of the sun on your chest.
The pinpoint and crescent beyond comings of judgment
to which I will show all my rainbow signs,
a rhapsody lighthouse from old structured rules
and bow ties who scoured our streets.
      If she says she loves the... way... I am

Love, dear love, I will never re-write you—
never capture you in scenes, moments, or landscapes—
never do anything but seek what you put first
 in morning nocturne hours—
never put codes on the markers and places
you show me—
still, unfiltered, beautiful and transitory—
elusive in your higher hidden laws
of green belly buttons and chains.

Elusive are we in the heretics' hour, love
I will never put you asunder.
It's gonna be, starting here... starting now

If the Revolution Comes, You Niggas Better Not Fuck With Our Cat (or, The Two Jerks in Love at the Conscious Open Mic)

In the midday when the revolution comes,
a tabby will scratch the circle drums
and an army of Hoteps
will break their dissonances
to stop and swat her away.
Cat daddies in dashikis
will stroll to snatch her
but they will draw back cuts and blood.

In the midday when the revolution comes
kings will chase her with their Tims.
Approximate nation times will be disrupted
as princes and kings throw their congas.
Voices of indolent African Gabriel's
will echo though temples and cathedrals.
Bugles and cymbals will break, blow and burn
and clang by colonnades of I's.
They will clang tone deaf by colonies of cries
while the willow creeks singe loud and long.
They will clang while the gladiators
Sweep and sweep the streets
yet she will scratch them, then howl and roar.

Sister Bastet, Sister Bastet coming.
Sister Bastet, mother of the 42 laws.
The struggle has bindings, cages and claws
and freedom has new sets of wraps.

*Revolution is a dissonance of Kente's and taps
and the sea is stole away in their grind.
Paradise now seems the lie of the mind.
Sister Bastet, Sister Bastet, coming.*

The Husband of the First Woman Punished by the Laws of Moses

The Eshel roots would not burn for him.
The snakes—aside his desperate recompense—
do not whisper, but circle up dirt clouds.
> *Take me from the caverns.*
> *Stone me by the mill ward.*
> *Crack the commandments on top of my skull.*
> *Boil my body in deserts and swamps*
> *till I have cleaned my subconscious of clean.*

The chill—though faint—unconceals the sunset.
The moon starts to figure every stone in Sumeria
but is invisible to bandages and eye sockets.
> *I have denied her; and now I deny the seraphs.*
> *I will junk the horns of Gabriel,*
> *every neck and every lute,*
> *till its sounds take no pretense of pleasure.*

The roosters crow, but cannot weep
as he roars at every fortified wall.
The roosters are immobile but sound is above lightning
in circular retraces and migrations.
The roosters connect to their various spirits
in polyphonies outside of his mind.
> *I have denied her. Now, I disfigured my gate!*
> *I bludgeoned myself as I need to be bludgeoned.*
> *I walk around the deserts with caverns for eyes*
> *and witness replacing vision.*

Portrait of a Practice Boy Spitting at the Gods, Hours After Thomas Finished
(after Sterling Brown's "The Odyssey of Big Boy")

Leave me be from Casey Jones, lord.
Leave me from Stagger Lee.
Leave me from such loudmouth niggas.
>   Death's taking a hold of me.
>   Death's taking a hold of me.

Leave me, lord, what is that sound?
Who broke your cornbread structure?
Who took my contrast between time and order?
That skeleton key's what is actual.
Who took my world outside my window?
>   Death's taking a hold of me.
>   Death's taking a hold of me.

Was Stagger Lee gone when they took my wallet?
Was Jazzbo loafing along the river Dan
when they made my body their mallet?
Has Brer Fox left me along with the rabbit?
>   Death's taking a hold of me.
>   Death's taking a hold of me.

Leave me, the world has made everything read
the siren has a disrupted echo
with the world in a rage. Every inch is a ghetto.
>   Death's taking a hold of me.
>   Death's taking a hold of me.

To swallow is artifice-pretense-night fall.
To plead my blood to an altar of steel
is to take in lead that will kill me.
My insides mutate and dream of the sea.
> Death's taking a hold of me.
> Death's taking a hold of me.

Leave me, I have to filter what is left of the river
what touch and time as transformed into fractures
  has blocked my sight and sky.
In the black, my body and insides cry
  "John Henry is a god who's a failure."
A big mouthed Buddha who lives in altars
of desperate men's secrets and plans.
Take from me this crutch of a steel driving man.
Take from me all but the real, and then
I will again here see to see.
Water, the spirits are drowning me again.
> *Death's taking a hold of me.*
> *Death's taking a hold of me.*

The Funeral Procession for Aunt Helen at Her Favorite Swap Meet

The train envelope's everything and nothing,
an accent-bass toned-over church bound cadences,
thick trombones dissonant
in the telling and retelling of exodus.
The continuum of Gabriel and the Northwest Unlimited
charges—recharges—cleaves and moulds
church bottoms upon bottoms
assorts them in stations, signposts and gates.

It provides a scale for her seashell man
calling with his corner horn
as his trinkets dance above the table plastic.
It is the pattern of her fry cook
and her breaded pagan altars
that delivered her from various deltas.
It is the choir for the bootleg man
and his trick bag of songs
Transparent and undeciphered.

And as the train passes the bridge and river
they move and talk of an elusive land
of quiet rest and impassioned sanctuary
in praise songs that run through the vacant lot
and about their entire bodies
their instruments—in a triangle, in triad, in unison
are played in their timbers beyond age and wear
as morning trains still head for a home.

The 15th and L Arsonist Who Threatened to Smoke Me if I Snitched on Him, 1994

As the new black inhabits
the morning air, police tape makes
a cyclorama out of his scene.
Organisms are painted
in the marsh and stumps.
The artist's mask of erasure
the creator that burned
and ethered his homeland
faces a life after acts.

From the gas can's mouth
all is fire and dramaturgy
yet no one will watch
his world burn. No holy
sepulchers to his pains
are made visible
and signs are not rainbow
but green and red. The Gods
of the morning commute
ain't got nothing going on
but the first week's rent.
Yesterday's rage made
into altar calls of flame
are rote in their muscle memories.

Light hits, and the sun clears
away all myth. Buses blend

into various traffics and stations
oblivious to his scenes. The boy
in his bubble of anger and wraths
looks down, then runs away.
In the morning, the pond
and it's newly minted caverns
obscures history only in its surface.

A Father's 20th Funeral Anniversary

Aside no church, thugs hear invisible chimes
and yellow tape fluttering in the leaves.
The old man's dust
recolors everything around it
in an oblong powder light.

By the fence, the dope boys
barely make their stomps.
Unresponsive service lines
do not move in cadences
but away and straight off buses.
Quarter words of sayers
transposed with heretics
are a blur past layers of dirts.

The old man claps, and particles
become a flock of nightbirds.
Ruins of a playground
are not ruins nor a playground.
The arcs of the busted jungle gym
lift and resheath their metal swords.
and the swing set chain stops its hanging.
Yellow flags flutter above the hill
       and the jetstream
and piles on the sidewalk give witness.

In chalk, the old man makes his ash interact
the bounce off rock after rocks
smoke sieves and reforms

among disjointed bricks
as the dope boys leer around, nervous.

At night, the chalk line
is body-grained specter.
A sister lays her rosary beads.
In a vestibule of space after space
Dope boys are awash
in their root keys to a land
where they cannot think anymore.
White sage sinks to become burnt out strands

and them niggas fall to the floor.

Old Shermed Pirus Who Struggle to See the Sun in Winter

Under a brass monkey sun
they reinterpret time
in space devoid of capital
old painters who sketch
Sunday winter elegies
in proofs of ice and black water.

With a hit of that, everything gray
becomes a canvas.
Battlefields reimagined
come alive at the end
of a stoplight in the median of shacks.
Re-enactments and uniforms
lose their shades and their lints
and battlefields are blunted from all purpose.

With every spin and shake
of the blunt and the bottle
the short days get warmer and longer.
Homies shoot dice with them
and beat back their pours.
Low riders fly above ground and their speakers.
Mama's calls are clearer
and not in the background
of every echo, sight in sound.

In winter, the rain punishes them.
It sweeps past the cops and the first aged startups.

It sweeps past casualties imagined and threatened
to the steps of childhood haunts.
The weeds that told of old factory remnants
are too cold to hold them in December.

When the OG Took the Fall for Once (Then Realized It Was His Last)

In the autumn of his (thirty-) third strike
thirty-three homies deny his name quick.
Thirty-three cutlasses (with runner dads) lock
him from the market but not the traps.
In the hour, D-boy in the round up looked
for penance but his scrubs were so still
among the brown boys against ivy walls
and gray cedars, there was no penance root.
In the not-jack out of all his jacks
he was dragged—on the ground and pavement—against
his will but not his karma debts.
The glass starts to shut out all rain and skies
and his cherubin cheeks betray him.
Forgiveness and its compound homes
are a transparent flock of shadows.
Corner stores are razed and destroyed, then
the window suffocates all light.
The steeple leaves, and then the cross flies.
And his cheeks are mush in dark windows
    "Homeboy, where did you go?"

Portrait of an Ex-Piru, Right Outside the Mall, With His Daughters Fixed High Heels

By brakes, old things are made new in neon.
A trap man's trick bag is a veil to his face
as the boys break his face in December.
By breaks, are the hands that never held cornrows
boxes that held moon braying of bricks
but never corsets or certificates.
Never the book bag or the 50 sack lunches
or the swap meet scrunchie band.
He holds her shoes in trap money bounds
but her smile is as willed as her hand.

Above, the boys in yesterday's paints
sag over her. The heckle and leer
over the surface of the Penneys sign.
They wash the what whiter, unbuckle their belts
then grab their dicks from the railing.

Strengthened foundations are never final.
Fervent attempts to turn back their skies
       are as hard as pavement on sales week.
The place—and block—and circumstance
       she has to leave him for.
"Hey old nigga. Why you cryin'?"
       "I hope, you'll never know."

Young Elder Who Makes a Scrunchie on the Sidewalk
(after Yeats's "Death")

Neither dread or hope
attend the bus stop grievers.
Many times, they've pierced out memory.
Many times, they fold up Walgreens symbols.
Till bonds become harder to break
till stitches beyond scars
both tell and show
of evidence of lost ones unseen.

Pieces of her side jacket
cuts of his gap-toothed smiles
before the dope god washed them gray.
Before hustling backwards
circled them a cradle of abstractions.

On the bus stop, man-boys recreate death.
Guts sag on underwears that await their ends
and gnaw at the frayings in their bones.
Guts sag on their skeletons without hones
yet their limbs still have the power to break.

Homies heckle her in the supersession of buses
but she pieces, knots, and cries.
Homies preen about as time passes on
but her homie's memory won't pass her by.

993

Because I talked shit.
Because I was fucked up.
Because I felt bad that his wallet
was at the record mart
and couldn't stand to see that braided girl cry.
Because I talked this big mess
before stumbling to her
 and
> "Robert, you're licking the grass."

Because she said I was scared of it.
Because she said I was scared of her
and wouldn't fucking listen
when she talked about her whack ass daddy.
Because I was scared of her
and was so scared of everything
and didn't want her to leave me
and situational ethics
caused me to do what she wanted
and afterwards,
> I told the boys on the bus

than nothing happened
and the blood was my busted tooth.

Uncle Moe Dresses Big Momma for Church, the Morning After One of Dad's Tantrums

And then the breast sleeve sparkles.
And collars have light again.
And the gold from his lockets
piece broken coat with ermines

and repainted devotion veils.
And rims are re-flipped,
turned to the side, pads
and waist talons are made

tidy and placed high and right.
Torn buttons and shoulders
worn out and broke are
put together in their pieces.

Soon, his rock-drills will reform.
Mania turned transformatively inward
will reappear as penitence in her room.
Clean hearts stated as evidence untoward

will make jagged her ceilings and hearths
in the flames that avarice and hunger feeds.
A fiend's credo is a thousand rewoven deaths.
The sewer line has a set of duties and needs

translatable only to her.

Pops Tries to Sell Big Momma's Special Pot for That Stuff

The elder's engraved pot rings in on the floor.
The dope fiend kneels before being escorted.
> *Dope man, dope man, where you gon' run to?*

A crowd gathers by the pavement.
An array of textured freedman's engravings
are refracted in the glow of the pawn lights.
> *Dope man, dope man, where you gon' run to?*

The circle journey from slave to freedman.
is flashed as engraved exoskeleton.
The circle journey from slave to freedman
is a concentric circle of rocks.
The shadow man has gazed too long at the abyss
and visions possess and shake him.
> *Dope man, dope man, where you gon' go?*

On the Day He Lost His Religion and Sobriety

By park dusk, tables erect
mirage shadow towers.
Upturns and kicks remake
his strung out bell rings
into noise that knows no thought,
unto sound that recedes
from no sieve or filter
in smoke, food, or liquor.
The lent fiend's penance flows
are empty in a park
that long scurried away.

"In gods austere then sober
I weighed my idols.
Take this recurred sparks
as my remembrance of clean
that was dirty to kids in the city.
Take these body pittances
of my mind as I bend
out all my pretense piety."

And at his last new days end,
he ties rope to spiked tree strands,
branches recut with stuff harder than words
kicks and upturns far harder than proverbs
rechaff the synapses in his brain.
They repeat failures from staffs
that broke too many mornings,

as whiffs that repeat again, then again
lights melt into sight—then sound—then order
to the seeker's dust bell's chime.

The Time He Wanted to Talk to Some Niggas at the Pier About Being a Kingpin

Bones—in freighted memory—shock
Bones, he calls on, as he's left by the dock
      but they respond too contrary to wants.
Ferry brothers, baptized in coke sweat,
      throw him—blitzed—into water.

Under ice, his masks wash, but they stake.
The prices of the spirits—in absence—are great
      as they dunk him in drug face by the shore.
Among food mixed with grains,
among grains mixed with scores
      the hoods de-baptize their debtor.
He does his buck dance under boxes of fire
      but they dip him in his dirt-glittered suit.

The fiend cries, and hoodlums laugh.
In babble, the junkie articulates half
      his descent past, his frozen face.
In ice, all burning tragedy and farce
are colonies that rejigger his cheeks.
Toll thugs ride off to continue their haunts
      leaving him in the water with his tongues.

Burning Unc's Poetry Papers

Fragments of masterworks—
Years worth of theories—
Failures intertwined
with a million unsung triumphs
disappear as they disappear
 over their gaslight.
The new death-by-fire
of a thousand interlinked cites
is magnified by kindles and sparks.

In this set trip, erasure
has a conclave in smoke.
The new breed of hustlers
on the grind and the take
have no traditions save dollar law—
have no heirloom outside the OG's jaws
and the abyss that his hunger feeds.

Yet, they blow and burn,
already just paper.
Oshun: long strangled
in simulacrum of the river.
Isis: long mummified
by a thousand woke altars
of a hundred Stagger Lees.
The OGs know
what the griot-boys can't see
in emblems passed as thorns.

Yet now, on the corner,
the flame has no parentage.
It asks no questions
of ancestry and heritage
or anything except immediate fact.
It judges in extremis—
a severe final act—
then leaves every origin to its ash.

Song for Mrs. Eulalah
(after John Dryden's "A Song for St. Cecilia's Day")

"In harmony, heavenly harmony
 in universal love"
                              they cry,
as nature underneath a row
    of preaching deacons lay.
(They would not adorn her head.)
Church folks' banish is heard on high
    "Mean old Mrs. McDaniels's dead."
And music, in its power to obey
order and stations, makes its leap
    but cannot leave or ground the dread.

What passion cannot music raise and quell.
    Yet sisters break their Concha shells
as angry deacons stand their ground
in irreverence. Her loved ones faces fell
    yet the choir comes alive in sound.

The trumpet blows but cannot summon Gabriel.
The mezzo sopranos speak of Ariel
    yet this hearth is an upraised altar
encamped against her on her side.
Her dying notes are never took in stride
    yet the beat calls the crowd to a fever.

But, lord, what can "the one" teach tonight?
What voice can bring now heat or light
    away from her heretical praise?
Apollo's cynicism that masks as sight

cries in its form over her wayward ways
>   but cannot disguise itself as love.

Yet the people need power, and there she lays.
The procession moves but not with the spheres
>   in her last and dreadful hour.
The church parlor pageant shall devour
>   but no bugles are heard on high.
The alive are still with us, the dead have died.
>   Yet no music here will retune the sky.

The Gun Solstice: An Anti-Journey
(after W.B. Yeats, Mahalia Jackson, Thomas Dorsey, T. S. Eliot, Wallace Stevens, Stevie Wonder, Carl Sandberg, The Staple Singers, and whatever nigga that I didn't credit for writing revelations)

"I think what happens now is we go up to Ash Street
and clean them out," Police Sgt. Sam Thrall said. "...
We have a real concentration of bad guys there and
the neighborhood has finally clashed with them face
to face. The fact that nobody got hurt—it is kind of
amazing," unidentified officer, September 23rd, 1989,
Los Angeles Times

*BANG BANG BANG BANG BANG BANG BANG BANG
BANG BANG BANG BANG BANG BANG BANG BANG*

*"I believe in god. I just don't like the nigga (that much).
He makes me lie down in concrete pastures.
He creates seasons—in bunches of metaphors—
That make all look like tombs and shadows"*

The last light of blue upon black in the sky
dies oh so suddenly by the lamp lit.
The earth is the Pirus' and everything in it,
in migrations and handkerchief fights.

The gunshot—tonight—is the final sign
past cop cars and shadow led outlines,
past boats without water, seas without waves
and rides without horses or skies.

Twenty-four hoods and twenty-four elders

make the block simmer hot like a bomb.
Twenty-four hoods and twenty-four elders
speak in syllables that blow off limbs.

Under stations with dozens of crosses
Bad Friday—past the rock house—now calls
the roll past the gunshot's dividing bells.
Under the sign of shells and empty magnums

holy gates lock and close. Under misaligned scales,
traps and domes, rage costumes in a million masks.
The tree of life is bare. Every room is sealed
and now you are stranded in the dusk.

BANG BANG BANG BANG BANG BANG BANG BANG
BANG BANG BANG BANG BANG BANG BANG BANG
BANG BANG BANG BANG BANG BANG BANG BANG

And the sky—from a distance is a liturgy of lead.
Sister's basket carries rituals of the head
that have gone through myriads of fields.
The hampers move through side streets like shields

as Georgia sisters move in sequence.
    Run, run, Homeboy, run.
    Ride to the city of refuge.
And Bangers move, oblivious to deliverance
and the comings of crystal pastorals.
Fiends/knuckled heads hear their own chorales

but the sisters move away from the spirits
sound and thunder strands both charged and passed
singe above them in contrasting judgments.

Run, run, Homeboy, run.
    Ride old Keds above.
Singe in the red of a sunset abyss

and their memories of clay and dark stars.
Singed, the rhetoric of diligence and work
invisible in twilight routine walks.
The spirit—in rock markets—doesn't know how to talk

and the carrier of their burdens lies meager.
    Run, run, Homeboy, run.
    Ride to the city of refuge.
Players, iced up lost sons and mothers
the lost baller players (and players
before them) travel in a wilderness of keys.

Displaced is the keeper of penitence and dreams
yet the sisters move north toward the sea.
        If I had two stacks.
            Ride old Keds above.
        If I just had two stacks.
            Ride old Keds above.
        I would get momma a big house.
            Ride old Keds above.
        A big ol' safe and wonderful new house.
            Ride old Keds above.
The sisters move north and home toward the sea,
    Run, run, Homeboy, run.
BANG BANG BANG BANG BANG BANG BANG BANG
BANG BANG BANG BANG BANG BANG BANG BANG
BANG BANG BANG BANG BANG BANG BANG BANG
And we will excavate the graves of your brothers and sisters.
We will pile up dream ones for combat and sports

> *We are the summer soldiers.*
> *We are mighty.*

And pile them on the intersections—corners—blocks
and pile them in scorecards, stories and tracks
and dead sanctuary strands.
> ***We will even take your dreams.***

Shovel them to rappers and fortunate soldiers.
Shovel them to the cripped out children of corn syrup
and the crip soul catcher on the hill. The step
of our soft shoe will cut to your healers.
> ***We will even take your dreams.***

And pile, pile them into our memory.
And pile them from new kills and old cotton bones.
Stack them into fibers that transform into chapters
that you pen among set battle cries
BANG BANG BANG BANG BANG BANG
Two generations? Ten generations?
As you wonder past the set fights
BANG BANG BANG BANG BANG
> *We are the summer soldiers.*

> *We will even take your dreams.*

BANG BANG BANG BANG BANG BANG BANG BANG
BANG BANG BANG BANG BANG BANG BANG BANG
BANG BANG BANG BANG BANG BANG BANG BANG
BANG BANG BANG BANG BANG BANG BANG BANG
The rock house shootout is its own season.
Niggas and vigilantes break-beat the air
with base flames of incandescent terror
complexions of mad dog fill the skies

and the streets are mirrors of commotions
shadows of battles and tributary potions
    flood every street block and door.
        Niggas will be cripping on that dark day.
        Po-pos will do nothing on that dark day.
Figures who set-trip surround here an island.
Niggas who set-trip multiply by the thousands

as the last neighborhood squab shall be a first—
as a hood's bang stratifies and stratifies the mind—
as hoods bang from sneaks to gate of their burning rides
    and junkies run to the rock.
        Junkies will be screaming on that dark day.
Silhouettes rise off kilter as a barbecue pit
becomes a mile long in fire, and blackened.
        Niggas will be shooting on that great day.
Silhouettes and bodies real and imagined
jump at the body and face. They fit

and transform all definitions of place
and transfix by their sharp sunken eyes.
Ghosts, yet alive, fallen to rise
in threshing floors imagined and traced

The refracted fury of unwearied eyes
    coats the real city in flames.
Fall, fall, niggas! Paradise is a lie
He has become a home for the demons
and a haunt for all the homies

a haunt for every unclean, detestable deacon.
 And the ripple of niggas adulteries
 Woe! Woe! Real nigga city! Dressed
 in red linen and blue uniform

you glitter with new and dug up bones.
Power is jacked by an awesome god
and precious memories linger too long.
Their sins have piled them on to heavens.

God has remembered nothing but crimes.
Tonight the plagues have overtaken all
    in the blood jubilee socials.
We are consumed by fire in the Piru pastorals
and fire is the burnt rainbow sign.

A lamppost to the thunder and the black rose of Charon.
A lamp post to the lightning on that dark day saying
    "who shall be able to stand"

I believe in god, I just don't like the nigga
that much
I believe in god I just don't like the nigga.

Drake's Progress (or, Why I Can't Cry for My Wannabe Gangsta Cousin Living on the Block Now, and Feel Like an Asshole About It)

Your final picture of him cannot lay still.
Revenge—in all its sophistries—cannot warm your heart,
and ice takes reincarnation in all forms.
Bred wolves and killaz make everything bedlam
and the sad boy has tears beyond tats.

What is a king to a god of caught weight?
What is a god to a man-boy defrocked of status
in a paradise he imagined but never saw?
In a Byzantium of bright shiny grain leaden picnics
in fields only safe in HD screens.
Poor houses are jumping from the block to the (food) bank
but the gilded trap boy roams in a stasis,
a trap-debtors prison of time and calumny
as functionless as corner spots are fluid,
as spun as the smoke and the lean he dreamed
but now becomes him like a nightmare.

Masses have snatched from him all that resembles gold.
Outfits—outlandish once—are now his smudged markers
across the dirt of his Alabama starter jersey.
Shadows that bedeviled you are in the whites of his eyes.
Black guards here replenish and replenish again
and the rich boy cannot leave the scene.
The mountain you climbed that he tumbled toward
is too dark now, and here comes the 8 bus.

L. L., April 7th, 3:17PM (TW) (or, When the Doctor Asked Why the Homeboy Stabbed Himself, He Responded in Stanzas)

Someday, my blood will never be a sunset.
Someday, my brain will not be used up.
Someday, I'll wake and know where the time went.
"The needle took her," the text message sent
so I pleaded my skin with scissors and cup.
Someday, my blood will never be a sunset.
Away from this world, her needle bent.
Away from life, I left, in drip by drip.
Someday, I'll wake and know where the time went.
I wanted to go. But what I meant
was I wanted to see her in one last trip.
Someday, my blood will never be a sunset.
Without her, everyday is lent,
everyday away from her arms and lips.
Someday, I'll wake and know where the time went.
In the wilderness I live-write-repent—
In wilderness away from death's sharp tip.
Someday, my blood will never be a sunset.
Someday, I'll wake and know where the time went.

Visit to the House After "The Accident"
(after Elizabeth Bishop's "Visits to St. Elizabeth's")

This is a house that will never get clean.

This is a boy
in a house that will never get clean.

This is a bucket
and a boy who scrubs
in a house that will never get clean.
This is a father waving and smiling
waving over the basement and bucket and boy
in a house that will never get clean.

This is big daddy holding her covers
holding her picture as the father is waving and moving
holding her aside the bucket and boy
in the house that will never get clean.

These are the voices that hold the boy's uncles
holding him as he claps liquor radiated hands
holding big daddy as he grabs to her covers
holding all past the father waving and moving.
Holding over the red, rust painted metal bucket
of the homeboy who scrubs
in a house that will never get clean.

That was her "leap" that defied all logic
that defied the silence in the voices of the uncle
that defied all the prayers in the radiated hands
for big daddy as he grabs her old covers

that defied all reason of waving and moving
over the hard metal bucket
of the homeboy who scrubs
in a house that will never get clean.

That was the fracture that veiled her face,
the veil of the leap that defied all logic,
the fissure that radiated all the moving hands
that grabbed and weeped on covers
that shook among the waving and moving
that rang and rang over the red metal bucket
of the homeboy who scrubs
in a house that will never get clean.

These are the floors untouched by reality
the veil of the fracture over her face
the ground of the leap that defied all logic
the threshing bottom for radiated, too fissured hands
and the soil for tears over covers
the base for all of the waving moving
the depths (lord, the depths) of the red metal bucket
of the homeboy who scrubs
in a house that will never get clean
and the radiated threat defying her sickness.

This is his smile's bad actuality.
This is the threshing untouched by reality.
For reality is a veil over her fractured red face.
A passover that defies all leaps and all logic
a fissure that broke all bonded living hands
and a plague of enduring tears and covers.
The father moves and smiles
over the small metal bucket

and the homeboy sees visions
as he scrubs Scrubs
     Scrubs
         scrubs scrubs
in a house that will never get clean.

Portrait of a Ferret Among a Divorcing Couple in a Gentrified Startup

The eleventh hour of their startup.
The couple argues then chases her
past thrice decayed wall layers
and the lacquered veneer of a floor.
The boxes and TiVos
they stored from each other
have imprints in dust motes and scrawls
have blasphemes on comic books
and loosely drank bottles.
The god's they loved more than each other.

She scuffs past the stir fry
the engraved engagement china.
She hides in the words
of their old college texts
then scuffles the picture of their band.
They kick and slap the wood and siding
but the layers turn to mold in their hands.

They damn her in nightfall
in autumn, in transit.
They damn him as they take
their past to their friends' cars.
They fixate on her, and for a moment
they are united together
but the light switch breaks their illusions.

The Revolution Cannot Hold You: Freshman Breakup at the Amtrak

The horn—to the partisan—is an equalizer.
It makes naked all pretense, bombast and nerves.
He kisses her—then again—then again as she swerves
to a train that gets closer and closer.
She hugs him—then doors open—then he loses her
in blends of parents, families and couples.
Old partners embrace their significant others
moms and dads form their kids in a line
that affixes and reforms—a mosaic of time
as he gazes from his stations and her windows.
They taunt him, reform as old apparitions.
They snatch them from pasts to enforced presents.
They screw up his scene and his transparent acts
to the subtext of his fuckups' distances.
They reshape to versions of he and her rewritten:
their apartment—study spot—shared graduation—
he and her together in the back of the train
that dissolves at the end of his revolution.
The horn—to the partisan—is a curtain signal.
Nation times ring but cannot hold or tell
him they love him or get off the tracks.

To the Couple, the Tree of Life Lives in Metaphor
(for Jessica and Eric)

It is their banks that broke the dowry,
their bonds that don't brace—or gird—or ply
or confine to walls and buildings.
There is a tree of life waiting for you.

It is your acts that continue beyond all Hamlets,
your beginning beyond meridians
that the blues mistake for ends,
your dawn in every sight and sense
in love's manifestations in symbols,
in love's ability to make past tense
      death, dirt, and the cycles.
Love's the spirit charge that transcends all idols.
There is a tree of life waiting for you.

It is your trumpet that will never be too loud,
your signal that takes the crystal from every cathedral
      and carries you a crown of the mind.
May it be the tone that bends the thunder
from dead lands with no life or center.
Hope deferred is a pavement in the literal
and the imagination broke and beaten.
May your love be that tree more ancient than Eden.
There is a tree of life waiting for you.

l Lets My Body Be
(… Cummings poem of the same name)

When god lets my body be
from each ripped wound shall sprout a tree
of fruit that exists only for you.
My rosary beads will make you a laurel
of crowns, medallions
and alleyway garlands
no one but us can see.

My love, let me be your unknown color.
Let my back beget an afro sun
that turns inner deaths asunder.
That recolors all my ordinary worlds
into beauty from scabs of black
(that hold poisoned rivers).
Then, my love, I will swim into hell
and part out its ashen seas.

Love, our legs are a nation of labyrinths.
I want to wander with you
with no thought to go home
and no law greater than your conceit.
My riddles and scars
I will lay at your feet
and alchemize into acres of orchids.

A 2016 Jack Straw Fellow, Artist Trust Fellow, and nominee for a Stranger Genius Award, Robert Lashley has had poems published in such journals as *Feminete, Seattle Review of Books, NAILED, Gramma, Drunk in a Midnight Choir,* and *The Cascadia Review*. His work was also featured in *Many Trails to the Summit,* an anthology of Northwest form and lyric poetry, and *It Was Written,* an anthology of poetry inspired by hip hop. His full-length book, *The Homeboy Songs,* was published by Small Doggies Press in April 2014.

Acknowledgments

I'd like to thank my mama, my aunties, the block, uncle Mike, uncle Robert, uncle Gerald, the young ones at #colored2017, all the homies and sisters who have kept me in Seattle, Bellingham, and Renton, and Small Doggies. Lastly I want to thank, L.L., Tanya, and Aunt Helen (Rest in Peace).

Other titles available from
SMALL DOGGIES PRESS

The Homeboy Songs is Robert Lashley's complex homage to the black community of Tacoma, Washington. As part of a Northwest population with people from the deep South and a survivor of the Hilltop gang wars of the early 90s, Lashley's poetry makes sense of the multitude of voices that have surrounded him over the years. His passion joins high lyric poetry burnished by narrative structure, with a language attuned to the ear and the complexities of the human voice.

The Homeboy Songs
poems by **Robert Lashley**

$14.95 | 102 pages | 5.25" × 8" | softcover | ISBN: 978-0-9848744-7-7

"Robert Lashley is not just playing with a full deck; he's playing with all the goddamn decks. He trades in Shakespeare and Simone, Yeats and Dove, Auden and Three 6 Mafia and razzles and hymns, all with the kind of swagger and strut that asks and offers no apology. *The Homeboy Songs* is a stunning achievement, announcing Lashley not just as an important poetic voice, but as a new kind of prophet, one offering vivid visions not of the future, but of the vast sparkling Now. His poems are charged and smart and smarting; they seduce and hiss; they are, above all, incredibly potent, and incredibly necessary. Look, they say. This is how to look directly into the sun without going blind. This is how to live without flinching."
—**MINDY NETTIFEE**, author of *Rise of the Trust Fall* and *Glitter in the Blood*

"Whether on-stage or on-the-page, Robert Lashley's poems are about voice. His is a sophisticated voice driven by passion, and supported by both intellect and structure. Few poets can equal the power and originality of *The Homeboy Songs*."
—**JAMES BERTOLINO**, author of *Every Wound Has A Rhythm*

Other titles available from
SMALL DOGGIES PRESS

Into the Dark & Emptying Field is an interrogation of loneliness and its many masks. It explores innocence as the price of knowledge in a host of voices that share an emotional truth. McKibbens offers a monument of understanding for even the bleakest pieces of our human conundrum.

Into the Dark & Emptying Field
poems by **Rachel McKibbens**

$14.95 | 88 pages | 5.5" × 8.5" | softcover | ISBN: 978-0-9848744-3-9

"Hard and as real as the ax blade, the poems in *Into the Dark & Emptying Field* are unapologetically fierce and undeniably gorgeous. Strikingly imaginative and expertly crafted, these necessary poems shine a dubious flashlight on both the menace and the marvel that surrounds us. Otherworldly and at times shockingly brutal, McKibbens' work is both crucial and addictive."

—Ada Limón

"Rachel McKibbens' work shatters me and my world, then pieces us back together on the page like no other poetry I have ever read, creating a new reality, a self that feels what I cannot feel, sees what I cannot see. These poems are at once dreamscapes and yet as solid and real as stones in my hands, stones I want to press against my chest forever, then hurl back into the infinity of space where words of such beauty and power surely come from."

—Richard Blanco

"The ancient Japanese swordsmiths categorized a sword by how many body parts it could pass through, i.e., a two-neck sword, a three-arm sword...The strongest and deadliest was a four-torso sword. This book is a four-torso sword. You will feel it, hard."

—Jennifer L. Knox

Other titles available from
SMALL DOGGIES PRESS

Stevie Edwards's *Humanly* bravely and vulnerably confronts the complexities of living with mental illness in a voice that is equally feral and crafted. Through a gorgeous and gorge-filled landscape, these poems struggle with dislocation, past sexual trauma, grief, the chronic looming of psychiatric wards, and a constant attempt to redirect patterns of suicidal ideation.

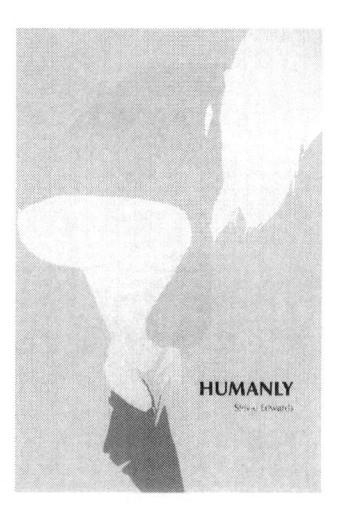

Humanly

poems by **Stevie Edwards**

$14.95 | 146 pages | 5.5" × 8.25" | softcover | ISBN: 9978-0-9848744-8-4

"If I had never before heard anyone say, 'Art Saves Lives,' I swear on the bullseye of my own wrist, I would have run through the streets screaming it the moment I finished this book. I want everyone who has never believed in the possibility of being given back Time, to read these poems. Not a moment of grief denied, and still, each turn of the page, a vaulted ceiling in my heavy heart. What a generous and intensely vulnerable offering to our survival this book is."
—**Andrea Gibson**

"With an unpredictability that alternately jolts and mesmerizes, Stevie Edwards has crafted an intricate exploration of life as we'd rather not know it. There is much in these stanzas to jolt and unsettle—stark crafting and a relentless respect for the possibilities of word create a tension only felt in the presence of revelation."
—**Patricia Smith**

"In *Humanly*, Stevie Edwards wakes us into our own bodies with her fierce honesty: *The first time I tried to slip my outsides/I failed.* This is a courageous book of startling images and original voice that surges beyond the difficult questions."
—**Jan Beatty**

SMALL DOGGIES PRESS

Artful Fiction & Poetry For Lovers of the Written Word

Small Doggies Press supports, defends, and publishes the most beautiful, challenging, and artful prose and poetry that we can find. We believe that the author has all the power, and our job is to create a context within which they, and most importantly their work, can flourish and find the intelligent, curious readership that it deserves.

Small Doggies Press is a division of Small Doggies Omnimedia, LLC, an Oregon. Corp.

Visit Us Today:

www.smalldoggiespress.com